I Am in Christ
Meditating on the Scriptures

By Linda Patarello

Unless otherwise indicated, all Scripture quotations are taken from the *KJV Reference Bible*. Copyright © 2000 by Zondervan. Used by permission.

I'm in Christ
ISBN: 978-0-9896919-7-0

Copyright © 2013 by Linda Patarello

Editor: Daphne Parsekian

Published by Orion Productions, LLC.
P.O. Box 51194
Colorado Springs, CO 80949
Orionproductions.tv

These small books with scriptures that fit each theme are meant to help you learn how to meditate. Each scripture has my own meditative thoughts that follow. This will help you to understand the thought flow that can happen when you think on God's Word. As you begin to think and ponder on God's Word for yourself, you will find more revelation in the Scriptures that the Holy Spirit will reveal to you personally. I encourage you to read my initial book, How to Meditate on the Living Word. That will explain in more detail the process of meditation.

This book in particular will outline what it means to be in Christ and the promises that brings. We will be meditating on scriptures that speak of our identity in Him as well as those that will illustrate why He has allowed us to live in Him—because He loves us.

"I will greatly rejoice in the LORD, my soul shall be joyful in my God; for he hath clothed me with the garments of salvation, he hath covered me with the robe of righteousness, as a bridegroom decketh himself with ornaments, and as a bride adorneth herself with jewels."

Isaiah 61:10

This is in the Old Testament, yet it is very prophetic of Jesus. We can greatly rejoice in the Lord; we can choose joy. Soul, you shall be joyful in your God! Look what He has done! To be clothed with the garments of salvation is to receive what Jesus has done for you. He has forgiven our sins and put us in right standing with God; we now have peace with God. He is the one who did it by His grace. We could not do this for ourselves. He has covered me with the robe of righteousness. We are the bride which is the Church, getting ready for our bridegroom Jesus. He has made us beautiful. Philippians 1:6 says, "Being confident of this very thing, that he which has begun a good work in me, will perform it until the day of Jesus Christ."

"And by him all that believe are justified from all things, from which ye could not be justified by the law of Moses."

Acts 13:39

The law of Moses was the ten commandments. It could not justify us; it only magnified our sins. No one could keep the law; only one, and that is Jesus. As we believe in Him, by Him we are justified in all things before God. There is no more guilt or condemnation to those who are in Christ Jesus, who walk not after the flesh, but after the Spirit (Romans 8:1).

"Being justified freely by his grace through redemption that is in Christ Jesus."

Romans 3:24

Christ has redeemed us. He has redeemed us from the curse of the law. He did it by His grace. Grace is what you cannot do for yourself. No one can redeem themselves; it is impossible. He did it for free, out of an enduring love for us. I am justified freely just as if I'd never sinned. To be given His grace is very humbling. It shows His great love and mercy towards man.

"And not only so, but we also joy in God through our Lord Jesus Christ, by whom we now received the atonement."

Romans 5:11

God is our Father, the great and merciful Father. It is through Jesus and His work on the cross that we have peace with God—that we are adopted by God and that we now can have joy in God the Father. We who have been saved now have a right to come to God in peace and joy, rejoicing in Him as our Father. It is through Jesus that we now have received atonement, which is restoration and reconciliation with God.

"Know ye not, that so many of us as were baptized into Jesus Christ were baptized into his death?"

Romans 6:3

This verse starts out with a question: "Know ye not?" Don't you know? Don't you realize? Those who have accepted Jesus Christ as their Lord and Savior were given new life, but in order to have new life, one has to die first. He died for us all, but in His death we also died. We were baptized into life with Him and into death with Him. We now have a new nature that is one with God's Spirit. The Spirit of God lives in us, and His power and anointing are inside of us to stay, never to leave, regardless of how you feel. We need to awaken to this revelation.

"Likewise reckon ye also yourselves to be dead indeed unto sin, but alive unto God through Jesus Christ our Lord."

Romans 6:11

Reckon means to take an inventory, to estimate. See yourselves as truly dead to sin. You are for sure dead to sin if you are in Christ. But just as much as you are dead, you also truly are alive unto God through Jesus Christ our Lord. We look too much to the circumstances in front of us. 2 Corinthians 4:18 says, "While we look not at the things which are seen, but at the things which are not seen: for the things which are seen are temporal; but the things which are not seen are eternal." We should look deeper and see what God sees. See things as they really are, not what we see. We are alive unto God! We have the power of God inside of us that raised Christ from the dead!

"There is therefore now no condemnation to them which are in Christ Jesus, who walk not after the flesh, but after the Spirit."

Romans 8:1

Right now, this moment, there is no guilt. Any guilt that you are feeling is not coming from God. Because of Christ, He does not see you as guilty, but you must first accept Him. He took your sin on His back; He took your guilt and your shame. 2 Corinthians 5:21 says, "For he hath made him to be sin for us, who knew no sin; that we might be made the righteousness of God in him." When you are in Christ, you are dead to the flesh, so you have no need to walk after it anymore. Your flesh does not have power over you any longer, unless you let it. Your spirit is now alive, so you can walk after the Spirit of life, which is in Christ.

"And if Christ be in you, the body is dead because of sin; but the Spirit is life because of righteousness."

Romans 8:10

You are the righteousness of God in Christ Jesus. What we could not do on our own, Christ did for us. No one is twisting our arms any more to sin. We were sinners. We were all born into sin, but through the work of Jesus, we have been made saints. Jesus did it. When we get baptized in water, it is a sign to show others what has happened on the inside. We were buried and have been raised into new life in Christ Jesus. Old things have passed away, behold all things are new. If the body is dead to sin, so be it. If you put vodka in front of a dead man who used to be an alcoholic, how can he drink it if he is dead? Now the only way we sin is if we choose to. Now we are free from sin. Choose life!

"For I am persuaded, that neither death nor life, nor angels, nor principalities, nor powers, nor things present, nor things to come, nor height, nor depth, nor any other creature, shall be able to separate us from the love of God, which is in Christ Jesus our Lord."

Romans 8:38–39

The great love of God is in Christ Jesus our Lord. One reason is that Jesus is God. God the Father, Jesus, and the Holy Spirit are one. 1 John 5:7 says, "For there are three that bear record in heaven, the Father, the Word, and the Holy Ghost: and these three are one." God also loves his Son Jesus very much. God loves us the same as He loves Jesus. They are one, and we are one. There is nothing that can separate us from the love of God—nothing. His love is in our Spirit. We are one; it can never leave, for His Spirit is joined with our Spirit now. No death can separate you from His love. Not life, nor angels; no darkness, principalities, or powers can separate you from the love of God. No past, no present, no future can do it. No height, no depth can separate you. No creature, animal, or person shall ever be able to separate you from His love. There is nothing that you can do or have ever done that will stop God from loving you.

"So we, being many, are one body in Christ, and every one members one of another."

Romans 12:5

Think of the millions of Christians all over the world in many different countries: all of the diverse people groups with various races, colors, and languages, all coming from many walks of life—rich and poor, famous and unknown. All these make up one body with Christ being the head. In Christ, we are one. Each is a different member with different gifts and purposes, but we all need each other; we nurture and feed one another.

9

Without each other, there is no body. The same love is in each of our spirits. We have that love in common no matter how different we are. But it is because of Him. He brings us all together. He is our Lord. He is our head and chief cornerstone.

"I thank my God always on your behalf, for grace of God which is given you by Jesus Christ; That in every thing ye are enriched by him, in all utterance, and in all knowledge; Even as the testimony of Christ was confirmed in you: So that you come behind in no gift..."

1 Corinthians 1:4–7

Paul thanked God for His grace on our behalf, and that grace was given to us by Jesus Christ. We are enriched in everything in Jesus—from the words that come out of our mouth to all knowledge that we have been given. If you are saved, then His testimony has been confirmed in you. This truly describes His grace, for in His love and because of his love for you, He provided all that you would ever need in this life and into eternity with Him.

"Unto the church of God which is at Corinth, to them that are sanctified in Christ Jesus, called to be saints, with all that in every place call upon the name of Jesus Christ our Lord, both theirs and ours:"

1 Corinthians 1:2

Although this is about the Corinthian church, anyone who is in Christ is His church. We are the body of Christ. We also are sanctified because of Christ and are called to be saints. Sanctified means consecrated; to be holy is to be pure. There is no way we are capable of doing this ourselves. It is Christ who made us holy. We are called saints only due to the work of Christ. Hebrews 10:14 says, "For by one offering he hath perfected for ever them that are sanctified."

"But of Him are ye in Christ Jesus, who of God is made unto us wisdom, and righteousness, and sanctification, and redemption:"

1 Corinthians 1:30

Amplified:

"But it is from Him that you have your life in Christ Jesus, Whom God made our Wisdom from God, [revealed to us a knowledge of the divine plan of salvation previously hidden, manifesting itself as] our Righteousness [thus making us upright and putting us in right standing with God], and our Consecration [making us pure and holy], and our Redemption [providing our ransom from eternal penalty for sin]."

Every good and perfect gift comes from the Father. He is a good Father who takes good care of His children. He is a great provider and wanted to make sure that we would be taken care of spirit, soul, and body. He gave us everything in the physical and spiritual realm. Jesus is made unto us righteousness, sanctification, and redemption. It is because of Him we have these gifts. In Christ, I am the righteousness of God and have right standing with God. In Christ, I am sanctified and have been made holy. In Christ, I have been redeemed; by the blood of the lamb I am saved. I have been bought back to my rightful owner. He ransomed me.

"For who hath known the mind of the Lord, that he may instruct him? but we have the mind of Christ."

1 Corinthians 2:16

No one can teach the Lord; He is all knowing and all seeing. To see inside the mind of God would be incredible. But we, who are in Christ, have the mind of Christ. We have access to all the wonderful things God has provided. We don't have to rely on our own limited resources. He is the vast creator. He is the one who created and developed the atom. Lean on Him; this provision, as we trust Him, is a blessing to us and for us and for all humanity.

"We are fools for Christ's sake, but ye are wise in Christ;"

1 Corinthians 4:10

We are fools for Christ's sake. This is to say we take our eyes off of ourselves and become Christ centered. We humble ourselves and lift up the name of Jesus. In Christ, we are wise. We put our own wisdom aside, for it does not compare with His wisdom.

"For as in Adam all die, even so in Christ shall all be made alive."

1 Corinthians 15:22

Adam sinned, and this brought death into the world. Every person then to be born would be born into sin, which in turn brought death. And in the same way, as Christ was made alive, this brought life to all, if they would receive Him. All shall be made alive. Death came through one, but much more life came through the one, Jesus Christ.

"Now thanks be unto God, which always causeth us to triumph in Christ, and maketh manifest the savour of his knowledge by us in every place."

2 Corinthians 2:14

Be thankful to God for his generous benefits. He always causes us to triumph in Christ. To triumph is to have the victory. We must get our eyes off of the problem and the circumstances in order to do this (2 Corinthians 4:18).

"Jesus, when he had cried again with a loud voice, yielded up the ghost. And, behold, the veil of the temple was rent in twain from top to bottom; and the earth did quake, and the rocks rent; And the graves were opened; and many bodies of the saints which slept arose, and came out of the graves after his resurrection, and went into the holy city, and appeared unto many."

Matthew 27:50–53

What an amazing verse. This has so much to think and ponder on. When Jesus was on the cross, the very moment that He gave up the ghost the veil was torn. The gospel of John says that one of the last things that Jesus said was, "It is finished." At once God tore the veil that was in the temple. He wanted His children to have complete access to His throne and to be able to come to Him freely. In the Old Testament, only the high priest could be in God's presence. After Jesus died on the cross, no more sacrifices were needed; His was the perfect sacrifice, and now all could come to God through Jesus. When the veil was torn, it was torn from the top, which man could not do.

"For he hath made him to be sin for us, who knew no sin; that we might be made the righteousness of God in him."

2 Corinthians 5:21

God the Father is the one who made Jesus to be sin for us. It was because of love He made Jesus into sin. He poured the wrath that we really deserved onto Him that we might be made the righteousness of God in Him. He uses the word "might" because not everyone is going to take Him up on that. Many will not choose the love of God. Many hate God because of the spirit of the antichrist. He will let them go to hell if they choose, but many will choose the free gift of righteousness.

"Therefore if any man be in Christ, he is a new creature: old things are passed away; behold, all things are become new."

2 Corinthians 5:17

Your spirit man inside of you is a new creature if you are in Christ. Your spirit man was born into a sin nature because of Adam. We were all the same, and we had to receive Jesus when we first found out about him. At that time we became a new creature. God's Spirit became one with our spirit. A new creature is just that— brand new. Old things are passed away. That means all the past. Think of all of your past failures, mistakes, sickness, etc. You have a clean slate. Behold, look and see; all things are become new.

"I am crucified with Christ: nevertheless I live; yet not I, but Christ liveth in me: and the life which I now live in the flesh I live by the faith of the Son of God, who loved me, and gave himself for me."

Galatians 2:20

This first phrase sounds like an oxymoron, but it is speaking again about your spirit man. Your spirit man, the old sin nature, was crucified with Christ on the cross. Your new spirit, if you are in Christ, is the one who is now living; yet not you alone, but Christ is the one who lives in you. And the body, the life you now live in the flesh, you live by the faith of Jesus. He is the one who loved you and gave Himself up for you. He gave you His faith to live.

"There is neither Jew nor Greek, there is neither bond nor free, there is neither male nor female: for ye are all one in Christ Jesus."

Galatians 3:28

When we are in Christ, we are His body. When you bring all of us together who are in Christ, we are all His body—one body. Christ is the head. It doesn't matter who you are, or who you were, or even what gender you are. We all become one in Christ. We are one family, one body, one Lord. No one is higher than another. We are all loved equally. We need each other.

"For in Christ Jesus neither circumcision availeth any thing, nor uncircumcision, but a new creature."

Galatians 6:15

This new creature that we became when we received Christ is all due to His work and His performance on the cross. He did the work by grace and because of His love for us. We cannot brag about any significant work that we have done. It will not matter, and it will not match up to all that He has done. Remember, it is by grace you are saved and not of yourselves. It is a gift of God, not of works, lest any man should boast. The Old Testament law required that

Jewish males be circumcised. This was out of obedience to God. But now in the New Testament, speaking of Christ dying on the cross for us, that is no longer necessary. The old is done away with. Now we have grace. It is by grace that we are saved and live. No work or act of any circumcision can save you, only the sacrifice of Jesus on the cross.

"Blessed be the God and Father of our Lord Jesus Christ, who hath blessed us with all spiritual blessings in heavenly places in Christ:"

Ephesians 1:3

Jesus, through His cross and resurrection, provided everything we would ever need in this life and in eternity to come. Everything you see and touch was created first by the spiritual realm. Having all that we need in the spiritual blessings in heavenly places is primary because, through the spirit, you can speak forth by faith to receive of the physical realm. So having rights in the spiritual realm is crucial for subduing and taking our authority on this earth. So we can say, "Blessed be the God of our Lord Jesus Christ!" For He has done a great thing for us!

"In whom we have redemption through his blood, the forgiveness of sins, according to the riches of his grace;"

Ephesians 1:7

It is through the blood of Jesus that we have been redeemed. He shed his blood as an offering for our sins. He paid for our redemption in full. Nothing more is owed. You are free from the power of darkness. You are free from Satan's kingdom and from his hold. You are freed from hell forever. The precious price was high, but it was fully paid. All of your sins have been forgiven: past, present, and future. This is according to the riches of His grace.

"Even when we were dead in sins, hath quickened us together with Christ, (by grace ye are saved;) And hath raised us up together, and made us sit together in heavenly places in Christ Jesus. That in the ages to come he might shew the exceeding riches of his grace in his kindness toward us through Christ Jesus."

Ephesians 2:5–7

Jesus didn't wait for us to be good enough or holy enough to die for. He knew that would never happen. He loved us even when we were sinners. Even when we were dead in sins, God "quickened" us—made us alive—together with Christ by His Holy Spirit. By His grace you are saved. God has raised us up together with Christ (if we've been buried, then we've also been raised); God has made us sit together in heavenly places in Christ Jesus. If He is the head and we are the body, then we are sitting with Him at the right hand of the Father. We have been made joint heirs with Christ, so whatever He has inherited we are joint heirs to as well. The Father is full of kindness toward His children. He is going to show us in the ages to come the exceeding riches of His grace. The things we are going to experience are above what we can even imagine.

"For we are his workmanship created in Christ Jesus unto good works, which God hath before ordained that we should walk in them."

Ephesians 2:10

God is the potter; we are the clay. Isaiah 64:8 says, "But now, O LORD, thou art our father; we are the clay, and thou our potter; and we all are the work of thy hand." We are his workmanship, and He is directing our steps. Ephesians 2:10 says, "Long ago, God ordained that we should walk in good works, as we are in Christ Jesus. As we abide in the vine which is Jesus, as we stay connected to him, we will bear much fruit." We will walk in those good works, for it will be a natural thing. We have relationship with the Father, Son, and Holy Spirit. God's life will permeate our being. We are to realize his love for us as we meditate. We will be so loved that it can't help but flow through us onto others, thus bringing and bearing the good fruit. If we are disconnected to the vine, we will bear no fruit.

"But now in Christ Jesus ye who sometimes were far off are made nigh by the blood of Christ. For he is our peace who hath made both one, and hath broken down the middle wall of partition between us;"

Ephesians 2:13–14

When we were in the kingdom of darkness, we were so very far away from God, and our eyes were blinded; we were deceived. Because of Jesus and His death for us in our place, He has made us near to God by His precious and holy blood. He made peace for us with God. There used to be a wall in between us. We could not get to God because of our sin nature, so God came to us. Matthew 27:51 says, "And behold the veil of the temple was rent in twain from the top to the bottom…" God made this happen. The Spirit of God tore that veil. He did not want anymore walls between Him and His children. He is a good Father who wants His kids by His side. Through the blood of Jesus, we have no more walls. We can come close in peace now.

"For through him we both have access by one Spirit unto the Father. Now therefore ye are no more strangers and foreigners, but fellowcitizens with the saints, and of the household of God; And are built upon the foundation of the apostles and prophets, Jesus Christ himself being the chief corner stone; In whom all the building fitly framed together groweth unto an holy temple in the Lord:"

Ephesians 2:18–21

What a beautiful first statement. There is so much unity here: one Father, one Spirit—one Lord and one body. Through Jesus, we now have access; we have a way to the Father through the Spirit. There is no more distance, and we are no longer strangers. We belong to the family of God. We belong to His kingdom, and we are in his Household as citizens and as a family. Without Him, we are all nothing. We all are built around Him into a perfect fit as we grow together into a holy temple in the Lord.

"In whom we have boldness and access with confidence by the faith of him."

Ephesians 3:12

In Christ, we have boldness now, for we stand in Him. In ourselves we are weak, but in Him, we have confidence through our faith in him. The reason we have confidence is that we are secure in and sure of His work. We know He did enough. He shed enough blood. He took enough stripes on his back to pay for all of our sickness and disease. He went to the depths of hell as no one else would for us. Only He could do this, and He did enough. So we have boldness and access to God with confidence. Access means the right to approach and the ability and right to use.

"And be found in him, not having mine own righteousness, which is of the law, but that which is through the faith of Christ, the righteousness which is of God by faith: That I may know him, and the power of his resurrection, and the fellowship of his sufferings, being made conformable unto his death;"

Philippians 3:9–10

It is through faith in Christ that I have become the righteousness of God. Yes, we are the ones who believe, but even that faith was given to us by Jesus. So my faith and my righteousness come from Jesus that I may know Him. It is all about relationship; He is our friend, our Savior, our Shepherd, and our King. He is so much to us. He walks with us and gives us victory, even in the sufferings and persecutions that we experience in this life; we are experiencing some of what he experienced, even if only a taste. It brings us closer to Him; even in our pain we can fellowship with Him. We are conforming to His death.

"I can do all things through Christ which strengtheneth me."

Philippians 4:13

Alone, all I have are my own limited abilities and accomplishments, but when I am looking to these, it is very easy for me to become prideful. What are they compared to Christ's accomplishments? It is actually all right to see myself as weak and limited. For if I see myself as strong, I won't need Christ. 2 Corinthians 12:9 makes clear that when we are weak, He is strong; His grace is sufficient for us. All that He did on the cross for us was—and is—enough. It is His work, and it is His grace. I can do some limited things by myself. But through Him there are no limits as to what I can do. I can do anything He leads me to do. I must be Spirit led in life, for any other way is a waste of time. He is the one who strengthens me; He is my ability and my wisdom.

"But my God shall supply all your need according to his riches in glory by Christ Jesus."

Philippians 4:19

The riches in glory by Christ Jesus far outweigh any vast riches on this earth. Part of the provision of the cross is that Jesus died for our poverty. 2 Corinthians 8:9 says, "For ye know the grace of our Lord Jesus Christ, that, though he was rich, yet for your sakes he became poor, that ye through his poverty might be rich." He took on our poverty so that we could take His riches. It was a great exchange and in our favor. There is absolutely no need in heaven, for God does not have any need. The needs are here on earth. And this verse says "my God"— He is our God. He shall supply ALL your need. Not one need is left out. But there is a string attached; you must believe and trust Him.

"Giving thanks unto the Father, which hath made us meet to be partakers of the inheritance of the saints in light: Who hath delivered us from the power of darkness, and hath translated us into the kingdom of his dear Son: In whom we have redemption through his blood, even the forgiveness of sins:"

Colossians 1:12–14

Amplified:

"Giving thanks to the Father, who has qualified and made us fit to share the portion which is the inheritance of the saints (God's holy people) in the Light. [The Father] has delivered and drawn us to Himself out of the control and the dominion of darkness and has transferred us into the kingdom of the Son of His love in Whom we have our redemption through his blood, [which means] the forgiveness of our sins."

We have the Father to thank for this wonderful life. Give thanks to Him, for He has qualified and made us fit to be partakers of the inheritance of the saints in lights. We have an inheritance. There is so much to look forward to! We have all eternity to spend with each other and the Father, Jesus, and the Holy Spirit, not to mention all the saints that have gone before us. We are in the family of God! We are on the winning side—what have we to fear? We put too much focus on the devil, who has already lost. I want to show you a verse that speaks of Satan and how we will look at him in the end.

"I will ascend above the heights of the clouds; I will be like the most High. Yet thou shalt be brought down to hell, to the sides of the pit. They that see thee shall narrowly look upon thee, and consider thee, saying, Is this the man that made the earth to tremble, that did shake kingdoms; that made the world as a wilderness, and destroyed the cities thereof; that opened not the house of his prisoners?"

Isaiah 14:14–17

He has deceived too many, but we don't have to be deceived any longer. God has delivered us from the power of darkness and has transferred us into the kingdom of the Son of His love. We are in a new kingdom now, not just in the future. In the spirit, it is now. We should see it and use our imaginations to picture this that has already become. Look past your circumstances, Saint. See the light that has come. See His glory. His blood has brought us redemption. His blood has brought us forgiveness, even the forgiveness of our sins.

"For by him were all things created, that are in heaven, and that are in earth, visible and invisible, whether they be thrones, or dominions, or principalities, or powers: all things were created by him, and for him: And he is before all things, and by him all things consist. And he is the head of the body, the church: who is the beginning, the firstborn from the dead; that in all things he might have the preeminence. For it pleased the Father that in him should all fulness dwell: And, having made peace through the blood of his cross, by him to reconcile all things unto himself;"

Colossians 1:16–20

Jesus is one with God. Jesus has always been. He always will be. John 1:1 says, "In the beginning was the Word, and the Word was with God, and the Word was God. The same was in the beginning with God. All things were made by him; and without him was not any thing made that was made." All things—all things—were created by Him, in heaven and in earth, the seen and the unseen, no matter what they are, from thrones, or dominions, or principalities, or powers. And all things were created for Him. Jesus is before all things, and it is by Him that they are sustained. Jesus Christ is the head of the body, which is the church. He is the firstborn from the dead; He was the first to be raised from the dead and be born again. He occupies the chief place.

Philippians 2:8–10 says, "He humbled himself, and became obedient unto death, even the death of the cross. Wherefore God also hath highly exalted him, and given him a name which is above every name: that at the name of Jesus every knee should bow…" This pleased the Father. Jesus is the one who humbled his own self, and God blessed and rewarded Him and brought Him to the highest place. It was right in God's eyes for all the fullness to dwell in Christ. Jesus is the one who made peace for us through the blood of His cross. It is by Him that He reconciled you to Himself.

"To whom God would make known what is the riches of the glory of this mystery among the Gentiles; which is Christ in you, the hope of glory:"

Colossians 1:27

The promise of the Messiah came first to the Jews, but they did not receive Him. And so then He went to the Gentiles, which is everyone who is not a Jew, meaning you and me. What is this mystery that is comes from the riches of His glory? The mystery is this: Christ in you. The verse before speaks that this mystery was hidden for ages and generations, even hidden from the angels and men. God is brilliant and full of all wisdom. He is the one who chose to have Christ in us, the hope of glory. We needed to have His Spirit living in us while we were on this earth. We couldn't make it on our own. With Christ in us, abiding in us, and we in Him, we will experience fruit growing to feed others. We will be energized by His Spirit even as we are praying with the wonderful gift He has given freely to us. He lives in us. We have His life giving power in us, and this is forever and ever, Amen.

"For in him dwelleth all the fullness of the Godhead bodily. And ye are complete in him which is the head of all principality and power:"

Colossians 2:9–10

This first phrase speaks of the Holy Trinity. The fullness of the Godhead is Father, Son, and Holy Spirit. This fullness dwells in Jesus bodily. And we are complete in Him, which means the Father, Son, and Holy Spirit live in us as well. We are complete. You can read this in John 14:23: "If a man love me, he will keep my words: and my Father will love him, and we will come unto him, and make our abode with him." We don't have to understand it but just receive it by grace. We are in His family, and He loves us and wants to include us in everything. He is the head of all principality and power. There is no power that is above Jesus.

"If ye then be risen with Christ, seek those things which are above, where Christ sitteth on the right hand of God. Set your affection on things above, not on things on the earth. For ye are dead, and your life is hid with Christ in God. When Christ, who is our life, shall appear, then shall ye also appear with him in glory."

Colossians 3:1–4

Think of how you are a new creation, a new breed. Old things are passed away. You're in a new kingdom; all things are made new. Come into this new kingdom and find out about the new ways. They are higher, and there is freedom and grace beyond measure. You are dead from your old sin nature, and now your life is hid with Christ in God. He sits at the right hand of God the Father, and it is right and fitting for you to seek those things which are above where Christ sits, for you are a joint heir with Christ and you also sit in heavenly places. You should no longer set your heart on the things of this world. Once you realize how much you have in Christ, you will never want to go back to the old life; it will smell putrid and could never compare to the new life in Christ.

"I the LORD have called thee in righteousness, and will hold thine hand, and will keep thee, and give thee for a covenant of the people, for a light of the Gentiles; To open the blind eyes, to bring out the prisoners from the prison, and them that sit in darkness out of the prison house."

Isaiah 42:6–7

This is an Old Testament verse prophetic of the things to come in the New Testament. Now we can look back and see what has become because of Jesus. Here God is speaking to Jesus, "I have called thee in righteousness, and will hold your hand, and will keep you, I will give you for a covenant of the people, for a light of the Gentiles. To open the blind eyes, to bring out the prisoners from the prison, and them that sit in darkness out of the prison house." And Jesus did just that. He came as a light to us, the Gentiles. He came to make a New Covenant with us that would never end. He made the Covenant for us with God. He has opened our eyes and brought out the prisoners from the prison, those that sat in darkness.

"And the grace of our Lord was exceeding abundant with faith and love which is in Christ Jesus."

1 Timothy 1:14

Faith and love are in Jesus, and yet they are inside of us as well because Jesus is living in us. This is due to the fact that His grace is exceedingly abundant for us. And in His grace is all that we need in this life and into the next life eternal. Through the cross, He provided all of His never ending, exceeding grace. We are speaking of not just of any love but the God kind of love, which is agape love and unconditional. He loves us just because. And it's not just any faith. It's the God kind of faith. He supplied everything for us.

"Who hath saved us, and called us with an holy calling, not according to our works, but according to his own purpose and grace, which was given us in Christ Jesus before the world began."

2 Timothy 1:9

Way before the world began God had called us with a holy calling according to His own purpose and grace. This free grace was given by Jesus. He didn't only save us; He could have just done that, and that would have been wonderful in itself, but He gave us so much. God has done things on our behalf because of His love and mercy—because of His grace—not because of our works. We do good works not to earn our way but because we love God. We are not saved by our works. We are saved by His works.

"Thou therefore, my son, be strong in the grace that is in Christ Jesus."

2 Timothy 2:1

We are His children. He loves and corrects us in love as His children. He provided an abundance of grace through His Son Jesus. Don't be strong in your own strength or in your works and accomplishments. Be strong in His grace. If you are strong in your own works, you will not be strong in His grace.

"It is a faithful saying: For if we be dead with him, we shall also live with him:"

2 Timothy 2:11

Both should be strong revelation in our hearts. How can you live in Christ unless you have first died within? And if you be dead in Christ, shouldn't also be alive with Him? If you are in Christ, then you should also consider yourself to have death to the old man, the sin nature, your old spirit man; and also even more consider yourself alive in Jesus. Don't go back and live in the past, for your life is hid now in Christ Jesus. Look ahead to the future. It is bright, not gloomy. It is full of hope and glorious, supernatural wonders.

"But after that the kindness and love of God our Saviour toward man appeared, Not by works of righteousness which we have done, but according to his mercy he saved us, by the washing of regeneration, and renewing of the Holy Ghost; Which he shed on us abundantly through Jesus Christ our Saviour; That being justified by his grace, we should be made heirs according to the hope of eternal life."

Titus 3:4–7

The previous verse speaks of how we were disobedient and evil before Jesus appeared with the love of God for us all. He didn't save us because we were good, nor for our acts of righteousness, but because of His mercy. We became born again and regenerated in Him by the renewing of the Holy Spirit. He generously gave us the gift of the Holy Spirit. He justified us by His grace, so now we are as if we never sinned. He made us heirs with Him according to the hope of eternal life.

"That the communication of thy faith may become effectual by the acknowledging of every good thing which is in you in Christ Jesus."

Philemon 1:6

Beautiful good things are in Christ and Christ is in us, which means so many wonderful things have been given to us! It is very possible for you and me to have effectual communication as Paul and even Peter did in the book of Acts after the cross of Jesus. People knew that they had been with Jesus. They had the Spirit of God and the mind of Christ. We do too, but we need knowledge of His word. We need to find out what we have in Christ so that we can use it.

"Neither by the blood of goats and calves, but by his own blood he entered in once into the holy place, having obtained eternal redemption for us."

Hebrews 9:12

In the Old Testament, the high priest would offer up the blood of goats and calves for people's sins. Once a year they would offer up a lamb without spot or wrinkle for the sins of his people, but this would only cover them for a year. They were used to living this way, from year to year with animal sacrifices. We no longer live this way. In the New Covenant, we live under a new and permanent way—not by the blood of animals. It's a supernatural God way. Jesus entered one time into the holy place in heaven and shed His blood as an offering for us. Revelation 1:5 speaks of how He washed us from our sins in His own body. By this He obtained eternal redemption for us—the forgiveness of your sins past, present and future, are covered under this eternal redemption. Once you realize this, you will be set free from a sin-conscious, guilt-ridden attitude.

"Now the God of peace, that brought again from the dead our Lord Jesus, that great shepherd of the sheep, through the blood of the everlasting covenant, make you perfect in every good work to do his will, working in you that which is well pleasing in his sight, through Jesus Christ; to whom be glory for ever and ever. Amen."

Hebrews 13:20–21

God is love, but he is also Jehovah Shalom, which means peace. He is the one who brought Jesus from the dead. He is our great Shepherd, and we are His sheep. Through the blood of Jesus, God made a New Covenant on our behalf, an everlasting one. It is through this Covenant that He makes us perfect in every good work in order to do His will. He is always working in us that which is well pleasing to His sight. He is always looking out for your welfare, to bless and for you to be a blessing. And this is all through Christ, to whom be glory forever and ever. Amen.

"But ye are a chosen generation, a royal priesthood, an holy nation, a peculiar people; that ye should shew forth

the praises of him who hath called you out of darkness
into his marvelous light;"

You were chosen by God. You are in a different
kingdom. On this earth, it is backwards—people are
important according to how much fame or money they
have. In God's kingdom, everyone is important. Every
child of God is valued and accepted in the beloved. You
are a royal priesthood, a holy nation. You are different
than the world. We are deeply loved; it is all because of
Jesus that we have these benefits. We should not be silent
or hidden. We should shine! We should give Him glory!
We should shew forth to all the praises of God! He has
been generous to us! He has called us out of darkness
and into His marvelous light!

"Now unto him that is able to keep you from falling, and
to present you faultless before the presence of his glory
with exceeding joy, to the only wise God our Saviour,
be glory and majesty, dominion and power for ever and
ever. Amen."

Jude 1:24

Trust Jesus. Lean on Him and believe Him. He is
the one who has traveled so far for you and me. He is
able to keep you from falling as you trust Him and His
Word. He is able to sustain you. He is able to present
you faultless to His Father because you will be faultless
and holy in Him. He is going to present you with an
exceeding joy before the presence of His glory to the only
wise God, our Savior, be glory and majesty, dominion
forever and ever. Amen.

"Unto him that loved us, and washed us from our sins in his own blood, and hath made us kings and priests unto God and his Father; to him be glory and dominion for ever and ever. Amen."

Revelation 1:5–6

Jesus loves us. It was for love that He died for us. He washed our sins from our whole life in His own blood. He made the sacrifice. He is the champion of our souls. He didn't wash our sins in just any blood from an animal, or even a pure and clean animal, as in the Old Testament. That would have lasted only a year, like it did in the Old Testament when the priests would offer up animals to cover the sins of the people. He washed our sins in His very own blood. This demonstrates how deep His love runs. He was willing to give His own life for you. He could have left it at that, but He went on further. He is the one who made you a king and a priest unto God His Father. Most people cannot fathom this or have never even heard of it. What does a king do? He decrees orders. So you and I were meant to speak and decree His Word and to decree life. As for a priest, they offer up prayers and worship unto God. We offer up our lives as a living sacrifice unto God as in Romans 12:2.

About the Author

Linda Patarello is a born again Christian, and graduate from Charis Bible College in Colorado Springs, Colorado. She currently lives there, and spends most of her time spreading the truth about God's Love from the written Word. Linda is a California native with broad experience in leading praise & worship and songwriting. She believes that the highest calling is to worship the "Giver of All Gifts." She also believes we are born to pursue a relationship with God the Father, Jesus Christ and the Holy Spirit, and to share it with others. Her vision is to help people find true love for the Word of God, and to uncover its precious truths that are waiting to be revealed.

For More Information or to Contact the Author, Please Write to:

Linda Patarello
P.O. Box 7964
Colorado Springs, CO 80933

www.Heartsower.com

Prayer of Salvation

There is nothing more fulfilling in life than knowing that God loves you. God has made, and continues to make His love known to us by having sent His only begotten son, Jesus Christ, to die on the cross as payment for our sins and the injustices done unto us.

Has anyone willingly given up their life in exchange for yours, so that you may live? Jesus did. "Greater love hath no man than this, that a man lay down his life for his friends" (Jn. 15:13). Notice, that Jesus said this *before* he went to the cross. He laid down His life for us because he saw you and I, his friends, benefiting from this act of love.

You were the joy that was set before Jesus. "For the joy that was set before him [he] endured the cross, despising the shame, and is set down at the right hand of the throne of God" (Heb. 12:2). Only a true, selfless friend could love like this. Would you like to know the One Who finds you valuable, Who truly loves you? If you would like to ask Jesus to be your friend and your Lord and Savior, you can ask Him today. You can use your own words or pray,

"Lord Jesus, I want to know you, I want to be your friend. I invite you into my life, so that I may know you more. Be my saving friend, Lord and Savior. I am sorry for all my sins and past mistakes. Thank you for forgiving me and loving me, in spite of my past. You are my friend, even when I have no one else. I want to receive everything you have for me, even your Holy Spirit. Take control of my life, and through my relationship with you, let it grow and mature, and become a light unto others. Thank you for freeing me from sin and darkness, and for putting me in right-standing with you forever. I am saved! Thank you, Jesus! Amen!

If you prayed this prayer for the first time in your life, we believe that you are born again! Find a good Bible-based church, and connect with other believers. Please share your testimony or visit us online:

http://www.orionproductions.tv/contact-us.html

You can write to us:

Orion Productions

PO Box 51194
Colorado Springs, CO 80949

Blessings to you! From our staff at Orion Productions.

ori⁺on
PRODUCTIONS

*To make known the stories and accounts
of God's work in people's lives
through multimedia products and
services.*

*Our latest publishing information can be found
by visiting our website at:*

www.orionproductions.tv/publishing.html

www.ingramcontent.com/pod-product-compliance
Lightning Source LLC
Chambersburg PA
CBHW060640030426
42337CB00018B/3410